993.1   Higham, Charles
Hi
         The Maoris

993.1   Higham, Charles
Hi
         The Maoris

17530

The Maoris

Charles Higham

Published in cooperation with Cambridge University Press
Lerner Publications Company, Minneapolis

Dedication

He tohu whakamaharatanga
tenei ki nga tipuna.
Na to ratou maia me to
ratou mama i hoeatia e
ratou te Moana Nui A Kiwa
i kitea ai i whakanohongia
ai to tatou whenua
a Aotearoa.

LIBRARY OF CONGRESS CATALOGING IN PUBLICATION DATA

Higham, Charles.
The Maoris.

(A Cambridge topic book)
Includes index.
Summary: Discusses the history of the Maori people
and the effect of European colonization on these
original inhabitants of New Zealand. Briefly describes
the Maori today.
1. Maoris—Juvenile literature. [1. Maoris—History]
I. Title.
DU423.A1H53 1983   993.101   83-1856
ISBN 0-8225-1229-7 (lib. bdg.)

This edition first published 1983 by Lerner Publications Company
by permission of Cambridge University Press.

Original edition copyright © 1981 by Cambridge University Press
as part of *The Cambridge Introduction to the History of Mankind: Topic Book.*

International Standard Book Number: 0-8225-1229-7
Library of Congress Catalog Card Number: 83-1856

Manufactured in the United States of America

This edition is available exclusively from:
Lerner Publications Company, 241 First Avenue North, Minneapolis, Minnesota 55401

2 3 4 5 6 7 8 9 10 92 91 90 89 88 87 86 85 84

Contents

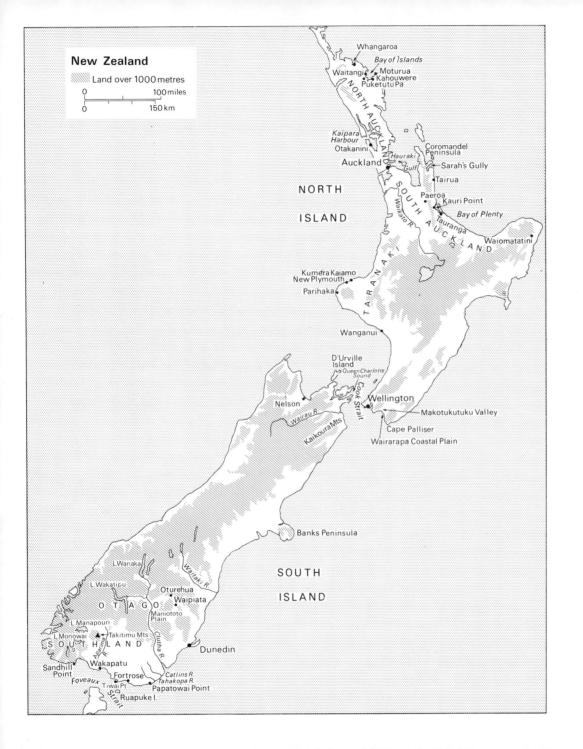

New Zealand

Land over 1000 metres

0   100 miles
0   150 km

Whangaroa
Bay of Islands
Waitangi   Moturua
Kahouwere
PuketutuPa

NORTH AUCKLAND

Kaipara Harbour
Otakanini
Coromandel Peninsula
Auckland
Hauraki Gulf
Sarah's Gully
Tairua

NORTH

ISLAND

SOUTH AUCKLAND

Paeroa
Kauri Point
Waikato R.
Bay of Plenty
Tauranga
Waiomatatini

Kumera Kaiamo
New Plymouth
TARANAKI
Parihaka

Wanganui

D'Urville Island
Queen Charlotte Sound
Cook Strait
Nelson
Wairau R.
Kaikoura Mts
Wellington
Makotukutuku Valley
Cape Palliser
Wairarapa Coastal Plain

Banks Peninsula

SOUTH

ISLAND

L.Wanaka
Waitaki R.
L.Wakatipu
Oturehua
Waipiata
OTAGO
Maniototo Plain
L.Manapouri
L.Monowai
Takitimu Mts
Clutha R.
Dunedin
SOUTHLAND
Aparima R.
Wakapatu
Sandhill Point
Fortrose
Foveaux Strait
Catlins R.
Tahakopa R.
Tiwai Pt
Papatowai Point
Ruapuke I.

Introduction

The first European drawing of Maoris. In the distance, you see Abel Tasman's vessels, flying the Dutch flag. Maori canoes are attacking a Dutch rowing boat as some of its crew try to swim to safety. The artist has given us a close-up of a Maori canoe. To the left, you can see the Maori canoes, one with a sail, pursuing the Dutch vessels as they depart. The drawing was made by a Dutch artist on Abel Tasman's expedition in 1642.

On 18 December 1642 a group of people looked out across the bay from their quiet beach. Suddenly two strange ships sailed into view. The watchers had never seen anyone from another land. Imagine, then, what it must have been like for them to see these two enormous ships approaching and perhaps to hear across the water sailors' voices speaking a language they could not understand.

They were used to warding off threats by fighting so they quickly got into their canoes. They pushed out into the bay just in time to see seven of the crew from one of the vessels embarking to come ashore in a rowing boat about the same size as one of their own canoes. They swiftly attacked the rowing boat and killed four men. They were pulling away when the strangers produced weapons which made a deafening noise and gave off much smoke. Small round balls of an unknown substance hurtled among the canoes and some of the men fell wounded. But, by then, the strangers were setting sail and leaving the bay.

These strangers were the crew of the Dutch explorer, Abel Tasman, who had been sailing eastwards when his look-out sighted land. He had noticed smoke rising and, hoping to encounter the native inhabitants, hove to in the bay to take a closer look. When he saw the canoes coming he took up his telescope to get a good look at the paddlers. He described the 'southlanders' as most skilful sailors, rough, brave and strong. They wore white feathers in their hair, and a square cloak tied at the neck.

After the attack Tasman set sail and left the bay. He named the place 'Murderer's Bay'. Over a century was to pass before more such strangers came to this land which Tasman called 'Statenland' and which is now called 'New Zealand'. It was not until October 1769, and this time the explorer was Captain James Cook who, in his ship *Endeavour*, had been charged by the Admiralty in England to explore the South Seas. He also described the people he encountered. Who were they?

1 Who are the Maoris?

Explorers like Cook and Tasman were often surprised to find the remote countries they visited already occupied. They wanted to know when the natives arrived and where they came from. There are two main ways of answering such questions. The first is to ask the natives themselves. To do this you obviously had to speak their language, and here was the first clue. Cook found that the natives' language was very similar to that spoken in the islands of tropical Polynesia. In fact, it was possible for a person from Tahiti to understand many local words. Perhaps the ancestors of the natives came from those distant islands?

Later on scholars came from Europe who could talk to the inhabitants. They found that there was no single name to describe them as a people. Instead, each person belonged to a tribe and each tribe traced itself back through a long line of ancestors to those who were said to have first come to the land in great sea-going canoes. Traditions tell us their names: *Tainui*, *Te Arawa*, *Mataatua*, *Kurahaupo*, *Aotea*, *Takitimu* and *Tokomaru*. Each tribe traces its ancestors back to one of them. Thus the Ngati Awa came in the canoe *Mataatua*, the Ngati Tuwharetou in the canoe *Te Arawa*. Only when the number of Europeans multiplied did the tribes band together and use the term 'Maori' which came from the phrase 'tangata maori' or 'ordinary person'. We will call their ancestors 'Maoris' in this book, because the modern Maoris and the earliest settlers were undoubtedly related. During the nineteenth century some Maoris called their country 'Aotearoa'. We will use this term, too, to describe the land when Europeans came.

The Maoris' history had been passed on by word of mouth until the Europeans came and tried to write it down. Scholars wanted to know when the famous canoes were supposed to have come. They assumed that they all came together in a great 'fleet' from Hawaiki, the name of the Maoris' tropical homeland. They listened to the priests who were trained to recite the names of their tribes' ancestors and worked out that the canoes might have come about A.D. 1350. But that was only a rough guess because different tribes listed different numbers of generations in their 'family tree'. It was also complicated by the fact that the Maori legends describe how the ancestors found people, known as the 'tangata whenua', or 'people of the land', already there when they arrived in Aotearoa.

There is, however, a second, quite different way of finding out something about the earliest settlers: this is by archaeology. Archaeology does not tell us the names of individual ancestors as the tribal traditions do, but it can help us to find out other things that the traditions do not describe, like how they built their houses, what they had to eat, whether they traded goods between different tribes and how they made the tools they needed.

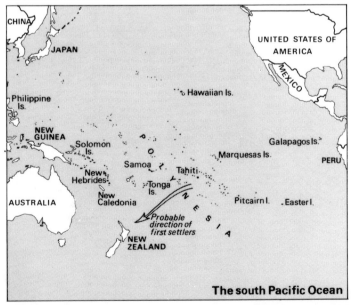

The south Pacific Ocean

Louis de Sainson's picture of two Frenchmen exploring the deserted Kahouwere pa in 1827. Compare this drawing with the one by a modern artist on page 17.

What can archaeology tell us about the early Maoris?

The archaeologist is trained to discover places where Maoris once lived, and to examine carefully what remains so that he can learn about their activities before Europeans came. Let us look at this picture of two nineteenth-century French explorers in a pa, or Maori fortified village, which had recently been deserted by the Maoris; then consider what an archaeologist, coming to the place years later when these buildings had all decayed, might be able to tell about what the pa was like and how the people there had lived. We can see the line of posts to help protect the inhabitants against attack, and the easily defended cliff in the left foreground. Notice the rectangular houses and group of low sheds in the distance. Louis de Sainson, who drew the picture in 1827, said that the timber

platforms supported on posts were to keep stored food away from marauding animals.

When archaeologists investigate a place where Maoris once lived or worked, they carefully remove the soil which has built up over the years. They collect all the evidence that has survived. They take care that nothing is overlooked or broken. Fragments of charcoal from the hangi, or earth ovens, are particularly important because scientists can calculate by a method called radiocarbon dating approximately how long ago the charcoal formed part of a living tree. Then the archaeologist can tell how long ago the place was lived in. So whereas we once relied on Maori traditions for the date of their arrival and settlement in different regions, we now have the evidence left behind by the earliest ancestors themselves.

Archaeologists are always keen to discover the remains of houses and villages, because these tell much about the size of

families and how people obtained shelter. They have developed a most interesting way of reconstructing plans of what were once wooden homes. Although the timber itself may have rotted or burned down long ago, the holes into which foundations were sunk survive as traces of darker-coloured soil. In the picture above, you can see the outlines of a rectangular house, with a stone-lined hearth in the middle. Since archaeologists are also very interested in what people used to eat, they search for old rubbish heaps. These middens, as they are called, were built up when people kept throwing the remains of their meals on to the same heap. Opposite is a diagram of a typical midden. Some middens contain only the remains of shellfish and fish bones and show us how the Maoris fed themselves when camped on the seashore. Others have only forest bird and eel remains.

As the archaeologist continues excavating the remains of such sites as Louis de Sainson's pa, he may find some fragments of stone and bone tools. Sometimes, the tools will be made of a type of stone coming from a distant quarry and this

will help the archaeologist to work out which people were trading with each other. There are times, too, when archaeologists find deep underground pits, which they think were used to store kumaras, or sweet potatoes, over the long winter months.

Archaeologists have investigated many New Zealand sites, and their discoveries tell us much about the land and people before first Tasman, and then Cook arrived. Let us see what they have learned.

The coming of the first settlers

We have already heard some suggestions about where the first settlers of Aotearoa came from. The Maori legends, their language and physical characteristics all seem to show that they came from islands of tropical Polynesia. Patterns used in Maori art, the practice of tattooing, and the similarity of tools found in Aotearoa and the distant tropical islands all point to the same origins. The radiocarbon dates from early sites in

There are two layers of food remains in this midden; natural sand has built up between them.

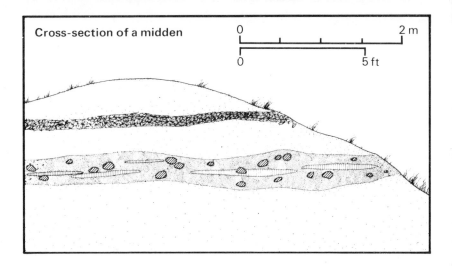

Cross-section of a midden

Aotearoa and Tahiti show that the first settlers came about a thousand years ago.

The Pacific Ocean is studded with small islands, some close to each other, others far apart. When the European explorers came they found people related in looks, language and customs living on nearly all the islands. The Europeans, being mariners themselves, were fascinated by Polynesian boats and navigation. The great canoes were hand carved from tree trunks with stone tools, and had sections of hull lashed together with strong rope made from coconut fibres, mat sails and wooden paddles. After generations of voyaging across the Pacific, the Polynesians were master navigators, using the stars, the direction of seabirds in flight, cloud patterns and the colour of the water as guides. We do not know what the earliest boats looked like, but the many crossings of the Pacific by early Polynesians suggest that the canoes must have been built to withstand heavy seas and been able to carry many people and their possessions over great distances.

Imagine the scene as some families prepared themselves for a voyage into the unknown. Perhaps there has been a dispute over land, or a growing shortage of food as the population rose in numbers. They pack their provisions carefully; there are dried kumaras, taro and yams. Rainwater and fish can be got on the voyage itself, but dogs and pigs are brought on board, some to eat on the journey, others to breed for food when they arrive at the new land. Seed kumara, a supply of fishing tackle and spare coils of rope are stowed away. Initially, the canoes

leave for the east; they know there is land there, because relatives have already headed in that direction and one canoe returned a few years later to describe it. But after a few days at sea, a storm scatters the boats and in the morning the leader finds his craft battered and alone. His first thought is to return home, so he turns back to the west. Unknown to him, however, the storm has carried his vessel so far off course that, in fact, he is sailing into an area with no islands for hundreds of miles.

As the days turn into weeks, the helmsman becomes increasingly concerned. Already, they have used most of the provisions. They have eaten all their pigs, and most of the dogs. Fish are scarce, and water is rationed. And still there is no hint of land. The sea remains a deep blue. There are no patches of seaweed or flights of birds to suggest landfall. Only a school of spouting whales breaks the endless monotony of the waves. To make matters still worse, the weather is distinctly colder than they have ever known. The helmsman's family and relatives shiver and seek shelter from the stinging spray.

But the following morning come the first hints: the sea is greener and colder – perhaps an offshore current? They begin catching fish more easily – can it be an offshore shelf of shallow water? Two days later and they see long, low clouds on the horizon, and a flock of shearwaters fly by. They recognise them as birds which nest on sandy headlands. Finally they see the land itself: Aotearoa, the land of the long white cloud.

2 Settlers in the new land

What would the Maoris have needed to survive in their new land? We all need food, shelter, and security from danger. In at least one respect the newcomers were fortunate, because as far as we know there were no other people to stand in their way. Nor were there any dangerous animals. As they explored first the coastline, and then the interior, they encountered a country thickly covered with forest. Occasionally, they recognised familiar plants: nightshade for example, which is called 'poroporo' in Maori, but 'oporo' in Tahitian. But the great, trackless kauri forests of North Auckland, the rich broad-leaved forest of the warm coastal regions and the silent and gloomy beech forests of the colder south would have been quite new to them.

Where were the first settlements?

If the traditions are correct, most of the settlers landed on the east coast of the North Island. Their present-day descendants will still take you to the very spot described in the traditions as the first landfall. The actual places where they lived are hard to find. It was so long ago, and there were so few people at first, that they have not left many traces. But archaeologists have found some early sites, mainly on the east coasts of the North and South Islands. It seems that the shores by the entrances to rivers were particularly popular places to live.

Tairua is one of these early Maori sites, probably being occupied about 900 years ago. It lies on the eastern shore of the Coromandel Peninsula. In 1958, fragments of charcoal, ovenstones, and broken bone were found when the wind eroded a sand-dune on the sheltered shore of Tairua harbour. You can see the site marked on the aerial photograph. A team of archaeologists excavated there, and found a deep and early layer containing many objects which help to answer some important questions about how the first settlers lived.

The site of Tairua lies on the sandbar (marked by the arrow). People living there could seek food from the open sea, sheltered estuary, and the forest, which would have covered most of the land in those days.

Aotearoa had very few mammals. Seals are native, but man brought the dog and rat with him.

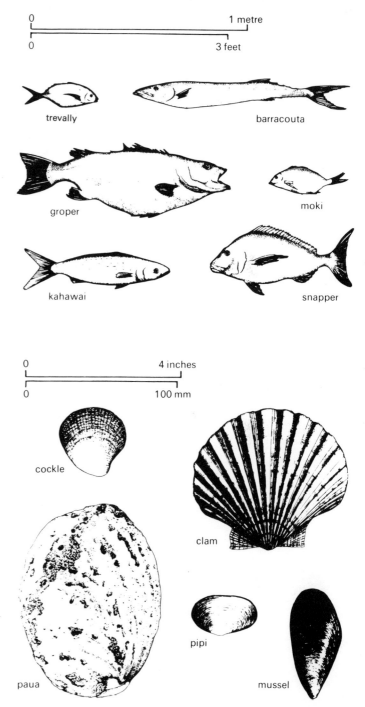

| 0 | | 1 metre |
| 0 | | 3 feet |

trevally

barracouta

groper

moki

kahawai

snapper

What did the early settlers eat?

Fortunately we can answer this question by sifting through their rubbish heaps at places like Tairua. Because these heaps contain bits of the creatures eaten, such as bones and shells, and sometimes also implements used to catch them, we can tell what the people ate.

The Maoris brought dogs and rats with them, as well as yams, taro and kumaras. But these plants could only grow in the warmest parts of Aotearoa so one of the first problems to be solved was what to eat. The coastal waters teemed with fish in the summer months: barracouta, kahawai and snapper came to their inshore feeding grounds in large shoals and could be caught with hook and line or nets.

As they explored the shoreline, the Maoris learned to dig for cockles and pipis at low tide, or flick mussels and pauas off the rocks. Seals came to breed in spring, and occasionally whales were stranded. River estuaries abounded with migrating eels during the autumn, and people living by the seashore would have seen many penguins, shearwaters and gulls.

Many types of bird were new to the Maoris, and they hunted them so much that eventually they died out altogether. The largest bird was the moa. Archaeologists have often found the bones of these birds in early Maori middens. There were at least seven different types of moa, varying in size and found in different parts of the country. The largest stood higher than an ostrich and the smallest was little larger than a turkey, but none could fly. You can see a picture of a moa hunt on page 22.

0   4 inches
0   100 mm

cockle

clam

paua

pipi

mussel

pigeon

weka

parakeet

oystercatcher

young mutton bird

These hollows were probably storage pits dug to store kumaras. Each one is about 2.5 metres (8 feet) across.

The moas were not the only birds the Maoris valued. Pigeons clustered around fruit-bearing trees such as the miro, tawa and kahikatea. Sometimes they ate so much, that they could hardly fly and were easily captured. Maoris learnt to place nooses over a water trough so that birds would ensnare themselves when drinking. There was also the flightless weka and the small, brightly coloured parakeet as well as the beautiful huia which were in demand for their plumage. This rich bird life made up for the lack of large land mammals.

Many forest trees bore berries attractive to man as well as birds. One such tree, the karaka, was found in coastal areas as far south as Banks Peninsula, and supplied not only edible fruits, but kernels which, after they had been treated to remove poison, were stored and eaten.

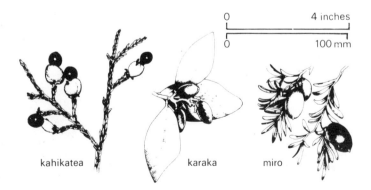

0   4 inches

0   100 mm

kahikatea   karaka   miro

These were some of the varied foods which the Maoris found, but did they also grow crops? This question is important because it tells us something about how many people may have lived in Aotearoa in those early days. People who have to rely on foods they hunt or collect have to be able to move seasonally to where the supplies of food are. But people who grow crops in their gardens do not need to move so much, and often gardeners live in much larger groups than hunters. How can we find out if early Maoris cultivated crops?

Archaeologists have found some clues at other early northeast coast sites. One of the most important is known as Sarah's Gully after the name of the last Maori to live in the area. There excavators found a series of six pits, each measuring about two-and-a-half by one-and-a-half metres (8 by 5 feet). A radiocarbon date suggests that they were cut about A.D. 1280. We are unable to show precisely what these pits were used for because their original contents have long since been removed. The excavators suggested that they were used for storing kumaras to keep them warm and moist during the winter. The difficulty is that kumaras simply do not survive long enough for the archaeologist to find them. If, then, we cannot find the remains of the plants, how about seeking the fields in which they grew?

In the early days of Auckland, European settlers described many large pa, or defended hilltops. On the low-lying flat land around each pa were field walls. But how old were the fields? Early European accounts of kumara gardens described how

This superb greenstone adze was found at Harwood, near Dunedin. It was probably placed in a burial about 800 years ago. Too valuable for use, it was made for display. Other more ordinary ones were made for clearing forest and constructing houses. This one is 40 cm (16 in.) long.

Greenstone tikis were worn on the chest by people of high rank. This one was given to Bishop Colenso by an east-coast Maori chief in the nineteenth century. It is 12 cm (5 in.) high.

the Maoris often burned the vegetation when clearing the land and brought in sand and gravel to mix with the soil. The ash made the soil richer, and a layer of gravel kept it moist. Therefore, the ash and gravel layers tell us quite a lot. One such combination was found by archaeologists at Moturua in the Bay of Islands. Charcoal fragments from the burned soil layer were sent to the radiocarbon laboratory for dating. It seems that the soils were in use by about A.D. 1230. Clearly, eary Maoris were gardeners as well as hunters.

Making use of the forest

The forest supplied many more things than food. The leaves of the karaka tree were valued for treating wounds. The berries and bark of the hinau tree were used to make dyes for decorating clothes; its gum was made into pigment to tattoo patterns on the skin. This practice of tattooing goes back to the Maoris' ancestors in tropical Polynesia—we know this because the bone tattooing chisels have been found there.

The nikau palm was found only north of Banks Peninsula; its leaves were made into many useful products from house thatch to baskets and mats. Its place farther south was taken by flax plants and the cabbage, or ti, tree. The inner bark of the ribbon wood tree was used in net-making.

The forest was also a source of building materials. Of all trees, the totara was most valued, because its straight timbers were the best for making houses, boats and carvings. Captain Cook noticed that the Maoris had no kind of iron. How then did they fell the giant forest trees and fashion timber into large vessels, houses and posts? They had brought with them from tropical Polynesia the knowledge of how to make tools from hard stone.

Stone for tools

Making stone tools is not at all easy. You must be careful to select the right type of stone. Some types break easily under stress. Others are too brittle, or soft. The first settlers must have been well pleased with what they found: there was a much greater variety of good stone in Aotearoa than in their homeland. One of their first discoveries was obsidian, a black shiny glass-like stone which can be given a very sharp cutting edge when properly chipped. But obsidian is of little use for heavy work on wood, because it is very brittle. For that, you need to make adzes from a less easily fractured stone, like argillite, which is found in many parts of the country.

Some early Maoris also discovered in what is now central Otago outcrops of a stone called silcrete. They fashioned long, knife-like blades from this. It took a long time, however, to discover the rare and beautiful greenstone, found on the remote west coast region of the South Island and in the mountains west of Lake Wakatipu. This prized stone was made into meres (a type of stabbing club), adzes and ornaments. A man who owned such things was very important. The man farthest to the left in the picture on page 27 is brandishing a mere.

13

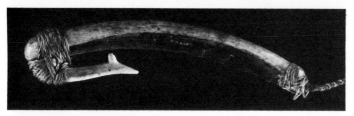

A fish hook, 13 cm (5 in.) long which would have been pulled along behind a canoe to attract barracouta. It is inlaid with shell to make it glint in the sun like a small fish.

Toothed implements for tattooing. The bigger one is 6 cm (2.4 in.) long. Notice how the chief's face in the picture on page 29 has been tattooed all over.

Stone drill bits like this one were used to make useful implements from bone. This one is 8 cm (3.2 in.) long.

What else did the settlers make?

What tools did early Maoris make when they arrived? We have seen above that they used sharp flakes of obsidian for knives. As wood does not survive for long unless it is buried in swamps, we do not expect to find many early wooden gardening tools, houses or canoes. Yet we can still describe many of the implements made soon after the Maoris settled in Aotearoa.

Among the finds at Tairua was a broken fish hook made from moa bone. It was therefore made in Aotearoa, but its shape is just like many known from distant eastern Polynesia. There was also a stone drill point and sandstone file, tools which were used to make fish hooks. Early Maoris also caught fish by pulling a brightly coloured lure behind a canoe. The lure was often shaped like a little fish, but concealed a hook. One such lure was found at Tairua. They also used bone for tools, such as harpoons, barbed spearheads and tattooing needles, and for ornaments. For example, they drilled holes in dog, shark and whale teeth, and fashioned large, tubular beads. The man sitting on the extreme right in the picture on page 27 is wearing a whale-tooth pendant round his neck.

Although archaeologists have not found early houses and canoes, they have found the great stone adzes used to fashion timber. Early Europeans described with admiration how the Maoris felled the giant totara trees, burned and hollowed them out into sections of canoe hull, and lashed them together before carving intricate designs and mythical scenes on the outside of the prow. The same adzes were used to square and carve house timbers, make storehouses and cut stout palisade posts.

Adapting to different conditions

We know from excavating many early Maori settlements that the descendants of the first settlers spread to most parts of Aotearoa very quickly. But as the country is about 1,600 kilometres (1,000 miles) in length, with high mountains, plains, tranquil river estuaries and rough, rocky shores, the Maori groups needed to adapt to very different conditions in various parts of the country. This situation was made all the more difficult by the great differences in climate. Thus the early Maoris were able to grow their root crops in warm, coastal areas in the North Island, but had to adapt their skills to become hunters and gatherers of wild foods in the colder south.

Cook estimated that nearly all the Maoris chose to live in the North Island. Yet some groups found that the plentiful seals, moa and fish farther south made up for the greater cold. In the next chapter, we will see what the archaeologists have learned about life among the northern Maoris. Then we will look at a fishing and gardening community located on the shore of Cook Strait before seeing how the Maoris lived as hunters in the far south. The way they adapted to their new world was different in each of these regions.

3 Maori life in the North Island

Archaeologists are able, by their careful excavations, to put the clock back and see what life was like when Aotearoa was settled by the ancestors of the present Maoris. Imagine that you can visit the Aotearoa of a thousand years ago. You would probably be struck first by the scarcity of people. As you sail down the Coromandel coast, the forest seems to come right down to the beach. On a still day, the air is filled with bird song from the dense canopy of trees. Seals haul themselves up on the rocks at the approach of a strange vessel, and gaze inquisitively and without fear as newcomers land. On the next headland, you see smoke rising. Here half a dozen rectangular wooden houses lie in a row along the forest edge above high-tide level. There is a small clearing within which some women are weeding between the rows of kumara plants. Other women look up to wave as a canoe sets out on a fishing expedition; they are collecting shellfish from the rocks for an

evening meal. The waters teem with fish, and already you can see that the men have hauled in two struggling fish, and are now trolling again.

The camp itself is occupied during the summer months. When winter comes, the families move to a more sheltered spot within the forest to meet their relatives. There, they live on stored kumaras and dried fish or seal meat. On mild days they hunt forest birds or moa. All look forward to the abundance of food which the first weeks of spring will bring.

Signs of war

For the first four or five centuries, the way of life of the Maoris in Aotearoa seems to have been relatively peaceful. This is not unexpected. A small population with widely scattered settlements would surely have little reason for strife, particularly when they had to grapple with the problem of adapting to a strange and, at times, hard new land.

By about 1450, however, the situation had altered. There were many more people, and the best land had been taken. The Maoris also had to face a serious new problem. Archaeologists have found, by analysing the calcite that makes up stalagmites in caves, that the climate became colder during the fifteenth century. The rainfall probably increased, and there were more southerly storms. It is true that this did not happen overnight, nor did it stop the Maoris from growing kumaras in the northern part of the country. Yet a colder, stormier climate would certainly have made offshore fishing more hazardous, and it would have made it harder to burn and clear the thick forest to make new fields.

It may, therefore, not be a coincidence that about this time some Maoris began to build defences round some of their settlements or move to new places, carefully chosen so that they could be easily defended.

Otakanini pa is one such stronghold. It is situated on what was once an island close to the southern shore of Kaipara Harbour. Archaeologists have collected enough finds and worked out radiocarbon dates to piece together a history of the site. They have pointed out the good sense of living there in times of danger. It is a naturally strong position and there would have been food nearby in the shellfish beds and fishing grounds of the harbour. The soils are good for growing kumaras. The area was formerly under forest, with rimu, beech and rewarewa trees and a ferny underbrush. Once the trees were cleared, the bracken fern would have spread. Its root was a favoured food among the Maoris.

People may have lived in the Otakanini area before deciding to build defences all round it. Indeed, the first evidence of human activity on the island comes from the fourteenth century, when a series of rectangular underground storage pits was cut into the sandy subsoil. At about the same time, a wooden palisade was built along a part of the island's coast that could easily be attacked.

Defending the pa

Perhaps it was felt that these defences were not strong enough because there was a second phase of building, this time more elaborate. The excavators found a series of post holes which once held large timbers sunk up to two metres ($6\frac{1}{2}$ feet) deep into the ground. They suggested that these posts once supported a fighting platform on which defenders stood to obtain an advantage over would-be attackers. The Maoris also cut a ditch and built up a bank of earth to increase the strength of their defences.

In the early sixteenth century, there was a final change in the defences. The occupants dug a long ditch the length of the southern defences and built a palisade of stakes on top of a bank on its inner side. Again, they built fighting platforms, like the one opposite, at strategic points along the palisade.

We do not know whether the defences at Otakanini were all built by the same group, or whether the earlier people were driven out and replaced by invaders. Certainly, the traditional history suggests that Otakanini was taken over by an invading group belonging to the Ngati Whatua tribe.

There are many similar pa scattered round the Kaipara Harbour although it is unlikely that they were all occupied at the same time. The people living round the harbour seem to have been very fortunate and so they may have found it necessary to protect their garden soils and fishing grounds from attacks by poorer tribes.

What happened if people who relied on the pa for defence in times of danger and for the defence of their harvests were defeated? The Maori legends tell of exile, of movement to new lands. The archaeologist can add to the knowledge gained from these Maori traditions, in the following way.

If you map the places where a particular type of pa with extensive bank and ditch defences is found, you will find that

they are mostly on the west coast of North Auckland, and along the coast of Taranaki and the Bay of Plenty. Probably, as the north got more crowded, people began to move south, taking with them their own style of fortification and types of storage pit. Finding the Auckland area well defended, they passed by the Hauraki Gulf, to settle in the Bay of Plenty and Taranaki. There they built new pa at such places as Kauri Point and Kumara Kaiamo. These movements then became part of the tribes' tradition. There are stories of invaders from the north, and even names of leaders such as Tamatea and Toroa.

We have seen that when Europeans first studied these legends, they concluded that the Maori arrived in Aotearoa in a great fleet of named canoes, including the *Te Arawa* and *Tainui*. Now we have another way of interpreting the legends:

In the foreground, you can see the terraced slopes of One Tree Hill, Auckland. This huge hill was occupied by Maoris long before modern Auckland grew up round it. Maoris moving south from North Auckland passed by the Auckland area because it was so well defended.

some canoes may have come from North Auckland, following struggles there for land, and the newcomers successfully settled in the fertile Bay of Plenty and Taranaki.

Wars did not end with these movements about 600 years ago. While the Maoris spent much of their time gardening, fishing and collecting wild plants, there were also periods of great danger, when the safety offered by the pa was vital. In chapter 7, we will see how the Maoris in the Bay of Islands defended their pa against a different kind of attack.

4 Life on the Wairarapa coast

About 900 years ago, Maori canoes rounded Cape Palliser, and headed westward through Cook Strait. The helmsmen closely scrutinised the northern shoreline because they were seeking new land to settle on. They liked what they saw. The hills were clothed with pigeon wood, titoki, miro and rewarewa trees, and, where streams flowed into the narrow coastal plain, the woodland gave way to kanuka, and karaka, interspersed with flax and ti trees. The waters were clear; there would be good fishing. A brief stay would be necessary to see if the soils would be fertile enough for kumaras, and to explore the forest. So they put in to shore.

In 1970, a team of archaeologists began to piece together the clues which allow us to find out what happened to those first settlers. It is not a happy story.

In this picture, you can see the shoreline where the first Maoris beached their canoes. There are few trees left, hardly any bush birds, no pipis or cockles, and not many fish, but there are many traces of earlier activities. There are lines of stone walls, traces of food refuse, pits and terraces. By extremely careful excavation of all these sites, the excavators revealed the rewards, trials and tribulations of life along the Wairarapa coast. Let us now see what it was like.

Establishing a village

One group of families has selected the Makotukutuku Valley, and begun to clear the dense vegetation along the river. The soils are easily worked. Forays up the river, flowing crystal clear through the woodlands, are rewarding too. They have already met many birds familiar from their homes in the north. The families have wisely chosen to travel in early autumn, because they will have time to collect karaka berries, prepare dried fish and lay in stores for winter. But most important, they will have time to make new tools and to clear an area for planting their kumaras next summer.

With the first hint of spring, they give serious attention to the question of crops. Their experiences farther north tell them of the need to plant kumaras in sheltered, sunny places, away from the danger of flooding or excessive drying out. They choose to clear the land on the higher part of the coastal platform, so that their crops are protected by a wind-break of trees. The forest echoes with the hammering of the adzes on the larger trees, and a plume of smoke ascends when they fire

This photograph of the Wairarapa coast shows a number of faint straight lines just above the hut in the foreground. These are ancient field boundaries, some about 700 years old. Compare this desolate scene with our artist's drawing on the next page which shows the first Maoris preparing their fields.

19

the undergrowth. Clouds of noisy parakeets rise, and settle again and tuis and bellbirds move away from the clamour. After the burn-off, the men begin to shift the stones and make boundary walls and pathways between the fields. They dig the ashes into the soil to enrich its natural fertility.

With the coming of early summer, the community sets to in earnest to plant out the kumaras. The men take their digging sticks to build up puke, or small mounds, to protect the tubers from excessive damp. They also spread a layer of gravel over their fields to prevent evaporation and keep soil moist enough for rapid growth.

Once the plants are in the ground, they turn to other tasks. Weeding has to be done but there is other work too. Long days of calm weather are good for fishing and, with another winter ahead, part of each catch is filleted on the beach behind the canoe-landing point and hung on a rack to dry in the sunshine. Armed with light bird-spears and traps, some men venture up the valley to hunt, while women dig for pipis, cockles and tuatuas at low tide, or take mussels from the rocks. On clear days, the snowy peaks of the Kaikouras are visible across Cook Strait. Some related Maoris there live near large flocks of moa. Since these birds do not live on the Wairarapa coast, moa bone and meat is in demand. They look forward to trading expeditions across the strait to exchange kumaras for moa bone or excellent argillite from D'Urville Island.

Soon, a regular pattern of activities developed, which changed little from year to year. Fishing, trapping and hunting birds, gardening and collecting shellfish and berries supplied their food. Life required hard work and with the passage of time one of the older men died. Soon after, several people were buried near each other at the mouth of the Makotukutuku River.

When archaeologists find graves with skeletons they examine them very carefully because they can tell a great deal about past peoples from their bones. The first Maoris in the Wairarapa were strongly built and led active lives. But few lived for more than forty years, by which age they had lost their teeth or worn them to the roots. We do not know the precise reason for such tooth wear. Perhaps it was caused by a coarse and gritty diet.

Hard times

As the generations came and went, life became increasingly hard. Consider the question of growing kumaras. After two or three crops the fields needed ten to twenty-five years fallow to allow the soil to regain its fertility. So greater areas of woodland were cleared. Fires may even have spread up the hillsides near the fields, destroying the vegetation and causing soil erosion. In some parts of the coast, great fans of scree spread over the remains of fields. Good land became scarce, and the Maoris began growing crops where soils were not fertile enough.

As the soils washed down the hillsides, the Makotukutuku stream bed choked with silt, and then floods brought muddy waters to the sea. This was disastrous for the shellfish, which relied on clear water, and for the fish, which fed on the shellfish and plants which once grew in the shallower waters.

When the soils were washed away, trees could not grow again and the forest-dwelling birds could not thrive. Like the settlers in the north, the Maoris here too suffered from the worsening climate from about 1450.

When we investigate the state of the same bountiful coast in 1550, then, we find a very different situation. The upper, more recent, layers in a midden have very few bird remains, and hardly any shellfish. There are still some fish bones, and we can tell that the people were still trying to grow some crops, but with increasing difficulty. Indeed, when you consider evidence in the valley itself, you find interesting clues. One living place was set on a promontory, defended by a stout stone wall. Farther up the valley were the foundations of a house built during these difficult times. The people living there had collected some karaka, hinau and pokaka seeds just before fire engulfed their house.

In a cleft in the rock near the defended promontory, the archaeologists found human burials. When X-rayed these bones showed the fine lines that are characteristic of retarded growth – clear evidence that the people suffered from a lack of food when young.

What, then, became of the people whose bones and graves the archaeologists found? It seems that their life became intolerable because of the colder climate. Poor crops, and strife over the little that remained, forced them to abandon their land. We are unsure when and where they went, but when James Cook sailed past the same shore in 1769, he saw very few signs of life.

5 Murihiku, the cold south

On a clear day, you can stand on the seashore at Tiwai Point in Southland, and look up at the snow glistening on the distant Takitimu Mountains. When the moist winds cover this country, they lose most rain in the high mountain chain of which the Takitimus are a part. So the west of Murihiku, that is the part of Aotearoa south of the Waitaki River, is very mountainous and damp. It is a hard country, much of it always under snow.

During springtime, some of the snow and glacial ice melts, feeding water into great lakes such as Manapouri and Monowai. The rivers then rise and the waters flow swiftly to the sea. The Clutha is the largest of these rivers. Fed from Lakes Wakatipu and Wanaka, it cuts first through a very dry central plain, where scorching summers follow icy winters, before it flows through a milder coastal area. The central plain is too dry for most native trees, but the damper coastal belt is thickly covered with beech and totara forest. In the Catlins area, it is particularly moist and many varieties of fern grow.

When the first canoes nosed their way into the estuaries of the Aparima, Tahakopa or Waitaki Rivers for shelter, they would have beached in one of the very best places to live in Murihiku.

The nearby sea took the sharp edge off morning frosts in winter, and the forest gave shelter from the cuttingly cold southerly gales. Fish and waterbirds abounded, and eels came and went on their annual migrations. When you walk along the seashore in Murihiku, you can often see layers of shell, bone and charcoal in the drifting dunes. These are the remains of early settlements. Some layers are thin and cover only a small area. Others are thick, and cover many hectares. Nearly all the river estuaries of Murihiku once had large, early Maori settlements nearby. Excavations have shown clearly that the people who lived in them were skilled hunters of the moa.

Finding food and shelter

One of the earliest known settlements is on the estuary of the Tahakopa River, at Papatowai Point. The radiocarbon dates suggest that it was first settled about a thousand years ago. The site lies within easy reach of excellent shellfish beds, and many pipis, together with a few cockles, have been found in the area where people lived. Being close to both the forest and the seashore, the Maoris were able to capture pigeons, as well as penguins, but most of their meat came from seals and moas. It is quite likely that the seals were clubbed while living in a breeding colony nearby. We know very little about moa hunting or, indeed, about the habits of these birds themselves. It is unwise to compare them too closely with another large, ground-dwelling bird, the ostrich, which runs fast and can deliver a deadly blow with its powerful legs. The larger types of moa may well have been slow movers, used to a peaceful life browsing among the coastal woods. They may also have been slow thinkers.

Imagine a party of Maori men, accompanied by their dogs, and armed with wooden spears, who have tracked down a group of moa near their nesting area. It is in a sheltered bend of the river, and the hunters move through the forest to cut off any line of retreat. Too late the giant birds sense danger, and huddle together in the muddy edge of the river. The men run in for the kill, shouting as they hurl spears and bring down clubs on the floundering moa. A boy collects the eggs while the men transfer the carcasses into the waiting canoes for easy transport back to the camp-site.

The women, some of whom have been collecting pipis nearby, come to help move the birds to the cooking area. All set to with a will: they hack off the necks and bony feet, and throw them into a rubbish heap. Then they take long stone knives and carve off the meat. Some is set aside for drying but they also decide to cook some joints that same evening.

The archaeologists who found stone blades scattered on the ancient ground surface like this were able to piece them together and get an idea of the block of stone from which the Maoris cut the knives. Each blade is about 15 cm (6 in.) long.

Archaeologists often find earth ovens, or hangi, like this one. You can see the hollow of the pit cut into the sand. Above that is a mass of stones and charcoal. The scale is in centimetres. Below is a photograph of present-day Maoris preparing a hangi.

Two men begin to prepare a hangi, or oven. They dig an oval pit in the soft sand and gather together a pile of fist-sized stones. They place dry wood and stones in the pit, and set the wood alight. Then they wrap the meat in leaves and fern fronds and place it on top of the smoking wood. Their next step is to cover the pit with earth and wait while the meat slowly cooks on its bed of hot stones. Some retire to the warmth of their wooden houses, others remain by the oven. It may be cold here at night, and it is impossible to grow kumaras, taro or yams, but there is plenty of food for the group, even in the depths of winter. When the weather is calm, they can paddle to neighbouring estuaries to visit their relatives, to share their new experiences, and exchange useful or cherished products. One community at the mouth of the Waitaki River has a supply of North Island obsidian for exchange. Our group at the mouth of the Tahakopa River has a surplus supply of parakeet feathers. So with dusk they prepare for their feast, and look forward to a period of good travelling weather.

Stone for tools

Archaeologists excavating in Murihiku found that the Maoris there had used silcrete for making their long knives, although none is found near Papatowai. To find out where the ancient inhabitants got it from they asked geologists, who were able to tell them where outcrops would be: in the uplands of central Otago. The archaeologists decided to comb the uplands for clues, and they found many. On a hillside near the village of Waipiata, which is on the edge of the Maniototo Plain, they found several artificial hollows in the ground. All round them little pieces of silcrete were scattered. This was a quarry where the Maoris had dug for good quality stone, and then made it into knives.

Over the nearby hills, they stopped at a similar hillside near Oturehua, and here was another quarry. Archaeologists collected all the fragments of stone left behind when the Maoris

The seashore in Murihiku. The men in the distance stand on the site of Wakapatu, a Maori settlement lived in about 500 years ago.

had completed their task. It was possible to tell where the stone workers had sat to remove the unwanted flakes and make long, sharp knives from the cores of silcrete.

During the summer months, about 900 years ago, it seems that some hunters, perhaps even those from Papatowai, had travelled up the Clutha River. At first they were only exploring, but once they found silcrete they began to quarry. They returned there whenever they needed to make more knives.

When the first few groups of settlers in Murihiku had learned how to protect themselves from the harsh climate, they were able to live very comfortably in their new land. They had good food supplies, and there were friendly groups of relatives along the coastline. Occasionally, some members of the community left for a few days or weeks, but life revolved round the home village.

Life becomes harder

Four hundred years after the first ancestors came to Papatowai Point, times had changed for the worse. The moa had become very rare; the weather had grown colder and more stormy, and there were more mouths to feed. How do we know about these changes? The bottom layers of the archaeologist's excavation at Papatowai had many moa bones, but the middle layers had very few, and the upper ones, none at all. When Cook came to Aotearoa, the moa was only a memory.

It is hard to estimate how many people were living in Murihiku at different times but most archaeologists think numbers increased because they have found more human remains from the later periods. There were still the warm summers but the abundance of summer food contrasted sharply with winter cold and shortage.

Imagine, then, that you lived in Murihiku five centuries ago. You would seek out places where crops grew wild in the summer. But you would have to travel farther to get enough to last through the cold winters. Let us look at the archaeologists' sites and see if we can find out how the Maoris moved about in their search for food. There is a site in the dunes at Kawakaputa Bay, known as Wakapatu. Some of the site has been badly worn away by the wind but one area remains, and in 1968 a team of archaeologists uncovered this part of the ancient settlement. Nearby are extensive outcrops of argillite, which, we have seen, is used in making adzes. Wakapatu is also close to the beach and when Maoris lived there, the woodland came down to the line of dunes.

We are able to work out what many of the activities were at Wakapatu. There are fish hooks which the people living there either lost, or threw away, and we can see that some were designed to catch the barracouta, others for smaller fish. There were many barracouta, spotty and cod bones found at Wakapatu. There are two large rocks on the seashore opposite the site, and these were covered by blue mussels. Clearly the Maoris liked to collect these shellfish, for many of the shells are found in the site itself.

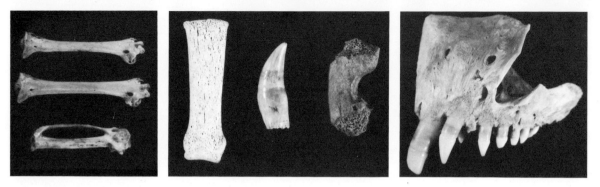

Bird, seal and fish bones found in the ancient site of Wakapatu. The jaw and teeth come from a small fish, and are 25 mm (1 in.) wide. The other bones are at the same scale.

When the archaeologists turned to the bird bones, they found the bones from 74 parakeets. These are brightly coloured orange-fronted birds and more than once, complete skeletons were found. This suggests that the Maoris plucked the feathers, but did not cut up the birds for their meat. The pigeon was the next most abundant bird (the bones of 19 were found), and in one part of the site there were 14 complete skeletons of the little white-faced storm petrel. Storm petrels live far out to sea in winter, and come to the shores of Murihiku only during spring and summer, from October to March. Unlike Papatowai Point, there were no moa bones at all, and very few seal bones.

When they were not bringing in food, the people spent some of their time making stone adzes. Many unfinished or unsatisfactory ones were thrown away at Wakapatu, but one reject had been turned into an awl.

When the archaeologists returned from their excavations, they asked several questions. The first was, 'when did the Maori live at Wakapatu?' This was answered by the radiocarbon laboratory: during the fifteenth century. Then they asked, 'what brought people to that windy, exposed shore, how many people were there, and how long did they stay?' Wakapatu is not large – at most it could only have accommodated four or five families. Clearly, they were interested in obtaining fish and feathers and stone for adzes. We have already seen that they must have been there during the summer, because they caught summer birds and fish. There is, however, a most unexpected way of being more precise.

When you cut a cross-section through a cockle shell and look at it under a microscope, you can see tiny growth rings.

These are made when the shellfish feed at high tide, so, in fact, they are daily rings. Now the cockle grows very slowly in winter, quicker in summer. It is possible by examining the pattern of the rings to tell approximately when individual shells were collected. Wakapatu was occupied, it seems, during March and April.

There are many other small sites along the shores of Murihiku. One is on Tiwai Point, at the mouth of the Bluff Harbour. Like Wakapatu, it was located near a good source of argillite, and fish, birds and shellfish were caught or collected. The cockle shells tell us that people lived there at some time between November and January. A third coastal site, called Sandhill Point, was occupied during December to February, and was used as a base for fishing expeditions.

So we can recognise a pattern: the Maoris travelled along the coasts in the warm months from late spring to autumn collecting surplus food. But where did they go in winter? When archaeologists excavated sites on Ruapuke Island in the Foveaux Strait, they found that the cockles there were collected during the winter. Ruapuke would be a good place for spending the winter because, being surrounded by the sea, it has no frost. Indeed, when the first Europeans described the Maori way of life in the late eighteenth century, Ruapuke was still an important winter home for the Maoris.

6 European explorers describe the Maoris

Captain Cook

Although archaeology has told us much about the Maoris, it does not tell us how they chose leaders, kept order, punished criminals, practised religion, or educated children. We can learn this only from the accounts of the early explorers who arrived before European ideas and tools influenced Maori society.

Some of the earliest accounts of the land and its people come from the daily journal which Captain Cook kept on his travels. After his first visit in 1769, he described the people as 'Strong, raw-boned well-made active people'. When he came back in 1773 he had much more to say about their way of life.

On Tuesday 3 June Cook's ship was anchored in Queen Charlotte Sound, when he saw a group of Maoris on the shore. He decided to visit them, and wrote these comments in his

Maoris in a war canoe, drawn by Captain Cook's artist in 1769. The men carry spears, also patu and meres, short, stabbing clubs made of bone or stone. Can you see the dog on board?

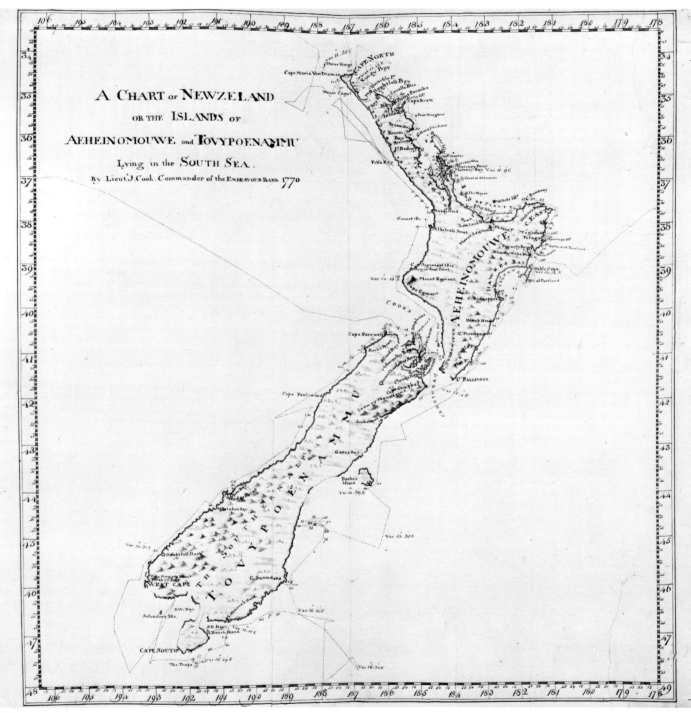

A CHART OF NEWZELAND
OR THE ISLANDS OF
AEHEINOMOUWE and TOVYPOENAMMU
Lying in the SOUTH SEA.
By Lieut. J. Cook, Commander of the Endeavour Bark. 1770

journal: 'we were well received by the chief and his whole tribe which consisted of between 90 and 100 people, men, women and children'. He noticed that they carried with them all their belongings, and lived where they found their food. Cook thought this way of life dangerous for he commented: 'Living thus dispersed in small parties knowing no head but the chief of the family or tribe whose authority may be very little, subjects them to many inconveniences a well regulated society united under one head or any other form of government are not subject to.'

Cook saw that the Maoris in the North Island had the advantage of strongholds, or pa, to retire to in times of trouble, whereas the South Island Maoris, 'by living a wandering life in small parties, are destitute of most of these advantages'. He did notice, though, that the southern Maoris did not need strongholds because, being so poor and mobile, they were in less danger of attack.

Because he came from a society with a king, parliament, detailed written laws, and the Christian religion, Cook was interested to see how the Maoris arranged such things. He found no simple answers.

It is important to remember that Cook and later explorers can only tell us what they themselves saw. We must also be very careful when looking at early explorers' reports. The very presence of a strange vessel, sailed by strangers speaking a new language, may have led the Maoris to behave in an unusual manner. Indeed, the Maoris thought that Cook's ship was a huge winged bird, and that the crew lived on it permanently. The different attitudes of the explorers must also be considered. After a long and exhausting voyage on the *Beagle*, Charles Darwin arrived at the Bay of Islands in December 1835 and described the natives as 'filthy, disgusting objects'. But Augustus Earle in 1827 was enchanted by much of what he saw. You can see some of his pictures on the following pages.

The Maori chief, Te Rangituke, painted in 1827 by Augustus Earle. Notice his elaborate tattoo and cloak. His wife sits beside him, and his son holds a musket.

This meeting between Augustus Earle and the chief Hongi took place in November 1827. Hongi's musket lies in front of him, and he wears a feather head dress.

Tribes and chiefs

Early explorers, even when they learned the Maori language, could only gain a limited understanding of how the Maoris lived and thought. Missionaries such as William Colenso, however, who travelled widely and learned the native language, came to recognise the presence of several groups of Maoris, each of which traced its descent back to one ancestor. They called themselves by the name of that ancestor. The Ngati Kahungunu, for example, were descendants of Kahungunu. These groups were called 'tribes' by the Europeans, who were accustomed to the idea of American Indian tribes or tribes of Australian Aborigines. Each tribe was linked with others, particularly if both were descended from those who came to Aotearoa in the same canoe; the Ngati Tai and Ngati Paoa are Tainui tribes, because their legends describe how their ancestors came in the canoe *Tainui*.

A hapu is the name for a segment of a large tribe. The members of a hapu are related to each other, or are adopted into the hapu by marriage. Large hapu may have several

Slaves preparing fern root for food. There is a European ship and several Maori canoes in the distance. Drawing by Augustus Earle.

thousand members, smaller ones only a few hundred.

Each tribe, hapu and family had its leader, but junior members could influence opinion by their powers of persuasion during meetings to discuss war, celebrate marriage, or mourn the dead. Early reports described how the tribes had chiefs, commoners and slaves. How did early explorers recognise which Maori was a chief? In the picture opposite you can see a meeting between two Europeans and the Maori chief Hongi in November 1827. You can tell Hongi by his dress, his commanding presence, and the respect shown him by other Maoris. Chiefs kept the tribal heirlooms, such as greenstone tikis and meres; they had elaborate tattoos and ornaments.

The oldest son of the senior family became chief because he was more closely related to the leading ancestors and gods. Chiefs commanded great respect if they combined generosity and bravery. They often had several wives, and lived in finer houses than other members of their tribe. They also had great 'mana'. This is a difficult word to translate into English. Essentially, a person with high mana is treated with the awe and respect due to superior birth and influence.

Members of lesser families were regarded as 'commoners'. These were free men, and had rights in their own tribe, but their prestige and possessions did not match those of the 'aristocratic' families.

The picture above shows a scene inside a Maori village in the Bay of Islands. The four people in the foreground are preparing fern root for eating by pounding it with beaters. They are slaves. The Maoris dreaded becoming slaves, because it was a permanent stain on their name and that of their descendants. War captives were sometimes killed and eaten, but some survivors were kept in slavery, and lost all their possessions, rights and mana.

This beautifully carved wooden haft with its greenstone blade would have been owned by a family of high rank and prestige. Notice how the eyes of the mythical figure are inlaid with shell. It is 45 cm (18 in.) long.

disposed of by any individual, not even a chief, without the agreement of all senior men. This attitude to land ownership became very important when Europeans tried to buy land, as we shall see.

Within the tribal area, land was owned by small communities of Maoris. They combined to work at gardening, fishing or collecting, and shared food within the group. But certain trees, shellfish beds, and flax plants were often owned and used by individuals, and were inherited by members of the same family.

'Aristocrats' often worked alongside 'commoners', but the chief had special rights, such as the products taken from stranded whales, and the first of the season's fish or kumaras. The chiefs looked after the family heirlooms, and owned most of the slaves. However they did not build up wealth, because being generous about giving things away was one of the main ways they gained their people's respect.

Keeping order

We have seen how the Maori tribes were led by chiefs, advised by a group of aristocrats. There were also the commoners and slaves. Early writers about the Maoris described the importance attached to personal prestige and the need to pay proper respect to other people and their possessions according to their place in society. Europeans were also surprised and often disgusted by what they took to be Maori cruelty. Captain Cook described the variety of Maori weapons of war, and took particular note of evidence for cannibalism. William Wales, who accompanied Cook, described how in November 1773 he saw a Maori cut meat from a dead man's head, and eat it 'with an avidity which amazed me, licking his lips and fingers as if afraid to lose the least part, either grease or gravy, of so delicious a morsel'. In the picture, you can see two heads being presented to an important woman.

Owning land

The land of Aotearoa was divided up between the tribes. Good land for gardening or hunting was especially valued and could be seized by a strong tribe from a weak one by a successful war. Tribal land not only provided food and raw materials; it was the resting ground of the ancestors and was occupied by their spirits. Many places were especially sacred because of events remembered over many generations.

Tribal land was divided between the hapu, with rivers, hills or even special boundary stones to mark the frontiers. This land was held by all members of the hapu, and could not be

After a clash with the enemy, two severed heads are placed before this woman of noble birth. Notice the captives in the distance at the left. Will they lose their heads, or become slaves? Painting by Augustus Earle.

English readers of such accounts were convinced that the Maoris were bloodthirsty savages, with no laws to control conflict. Yet, when we look more closely at the evidence, we find that the Maoris had all sorts of ways to stop dangerous conflicts arising.

Let us first consider a disagreement within a hapu or a tribe. As they grew up, Maori children learned what was good or bad behaviour. They knew that breaking the rules might well lead to the sorcerer making them ill.

What happened if a wife deserted her husband, or a man took food from a tree belonging to another? The Maoris had a system of punishment called 'muru'. The kinsmen of the deserted man, or of the person whose food had been stolen, were allowed to raid the home of the relatives of the wrong-doer. Even while these owners looked on, some of their possessions were taken. If it was a minor offence, only a few belongings were taken, but if the behaviour had been very bad, then many things were removed. The owners did not complain.

Conflict between tribes was much more serious. Each tribe kept a group of trained warriors ready for an attack, because stealth and surprise were important in war. In a society where a person's good name and reputation were prized, any insult given, whether intended or not, was sufficient cause for utu, or revenge. The same priests who looked after the tribes' history and customs also memorised past insults against their tribe. War was a way of paying back the insult and therefore restoring mana or prestige. Of course it was almost impossible to settle the score precisely, so tribes were constantly engaged in fights to restore their own good name and standing. Only if one tribe had a series of successful engagements did it seize another's land. Usually peace was patched up, by using the services of a 'peacemaker'. He was a very important messenger and it was tapu (forbidden) to harm him as he carried out negotiations between warring tribes.

One particular way of restoring mana and disgracing the enemy was to eat your war captives. Cannibalism does not mean that people were short of food, but rather that they were restoring their tribe's prestige in the eyes of others. If slaves tried to escape or disobeyed instructions, they were often eaten too.

above: *The chiefs of the Waikato tribe meet to discuss important business in the pa at Te Kaitote on the banks of the Waikato River. On the lower hill at the right you can see the ridges of an ancient fortified pa. The houses are built of reed tied with clematis stems. This drawing was made in 1846 after the tribe had become Christian. At the left is their chapel and bell.*

left: *This peacemaker had much mana. His tattoo is of the highest quality. Drawing by Augustus Earle, 1827.*

The gods and the priests

The early European explorers were Christians, and were convinced that theirs was the only true religion. The missionaries, like Samuel Marsden, came to persuade Maoris to forsake their ancient gods and become Christians. When these Europeans asked the Maoris about their religion, they replied that in the beginning there were Rangi and Papa, gods of the sky and earth. They had six sons, who were the gods of natural things: the sea, wind, wild food, planted food, the forest, and mankind. Tane, the forest god, mated with earth, and produced man. The Maoris then described how one early hero, Maui, used his grandmother's magic jaw bone to fish their country from the depths of the ocean. Some Maoris called the land 'Maui's fish'.

This store of knowledge about their origins and gods was learned by heart. The Maoris had special priests, called 'tohunga ahurewa', whose duties included memorising their sacred chants and seeing that they were passed on to the next generation. The priests and their religious rites played an important part in Maori life. They conducted rituals at the planting and harvesting of crops, communicated with the gods when there was drought or other natural disaster, and saw that the burial of chiefs was undertaken in the proper manner. The priests were able to lay spells on people who behaved badly towards their friends, or broke the ruling that certain tapu places, such as the scene of a recent death, should not be visited for a time. Priests therefore not only influenced the gods, but also encouraged people to behave properly towards others.

Caring for the needy

The Maoris believed that sickness was caused by evil spirits or sorcery, and the sick would go to a priest for help. The priest

Two Maoris drawn by George Angas an English visitor in 1846. You can see their woven robes, carved pendant and canoe head, and the man's tattooed face. The picture is the frontispiece of a book by Angas.

right: *Wooden house panel delicately carved with spirals and an ancestor figure.*

might ask his patient if he had been threatened by another person, stolen someone else's property, or broken any of the rules of tapu forbidding him to visit certain areas. Thus, if a priest had placed a temporary tapu forbidding visits to a beach where someone had drowned, then anyone going there would get sick. After finding out possible causes for his patient's illness, the priest would use his magical powers to drive away the evil spirits. If the patient returned to good health the priest's prestige would grow, but further sickness and death would mean that the patient's faults were too serious for successful treatment. If a person had an injury, such as a broken limb or deep wounds, the priest-healer would use medicinal plants and bandages to help the victim.

Educating children

All children learn by watching and imitating older people around them. Each society has its own way of doing things: Captain Cook was used to shaking hands as a form of greeting, but he saw Maoris rubbing noses together. And they still do when the occasion demands. Maori boys learned from an early age how to behave properly towards elders, and how to fight well. The Maori girls learned crafts, such as basketry, how to obtain, store and cook food, and how to present traditional dances and songs. The Maoris had no form of writing, so boys with the sharpest memories were specially trained to learn sacred chants by heart. It was essential to be accurate, because any slips would displease the gods and lead to illness or misfortune for the tribe. The brightest boys were sent for special training with the tribal priests. Eventually they would be priests themselves, able to chant their tribal history. If any boy showed particular skill at wood carving, or stone working, he too was apprenticed to an expert to learn the necessary craft skills. Therefore, although the Maoris had no formal schools which all children attended, they saw that the skills necessary for their tribe's well being were taught to each generation.

36

above: *An old woman weaves baskets and a slave (right) peels sweet potatoes with a mussel shell. In the background two old women greet each other outside the cooking house.*

left: *Women weaving flax into garments.*

below: *'Tangi' and 'ongi' are Maori greetings. When two friends meet they cry together for a while to show their joy. This is tangi (left). Then they rub noses, ongi (right).*

Three pictures from Angas, 'New Zealanders Illustrated', 1847.

All this information about how the Maoris lived before the Europeans arrived has been pieced together from the accounts of the first explorers. Now let us see how the Maori way of life changed when Europeans came to settle on their lands.

7 Maoris and the first white settlers

Once Cook's descriptions of New Zealand and its inhabitants became widely known, other ships called, some to explore and trade, others to make use of the country's natural resources. As long as the visitors were few and their stay brief, many Maori leaders welcomed the opportunity to trade. Europeans sought flax, seal skins and food, and timber for ship's spars. The Maoris prized iron, red blankets and muskets. But not all trade exchanges were peaceful. Contact between Maoris and Pakehas, as they called the strangers, at times involved misunderstandings and bloodshed.

The ill-fated voyage of Marion du Fresne

There was, for example, the ill-fated voyage of the French ships *Mascarin* and *Marquis de Castres*, both under the command of Marion du Fresne. In 1772, he anchored in the Bay of Islands to explore, trade and repair his boats. Three of his officers travelled inshore, and described Maori life in their diaries. Crozet drew a most interesting plan of a Maori pa, with its houses and storerooms. In one storeroom he found whalebone spears, clubs and wooden battle axes. The next

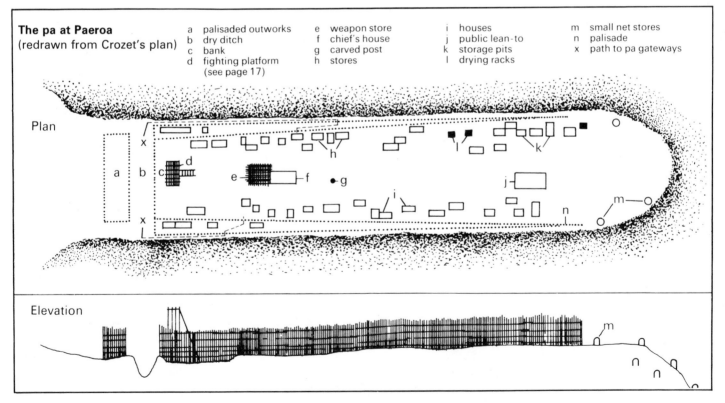

The pa at Paeroa
(redrawn from Crozet's plan)

a palisaded outworks
b dry ditch
c bank
d fighting platform
    (see page 17)
e weapon store
f chief's house
g carved post
h stores
i houses
j public lean-to
k storage pits
l drying racks
m small net stores
n palisade
x path to pa gateways

Plan

Elevation

contained sacks of kumaras and shellfish threaded on strings, while a third was full of fishing gear. Then he entered a house through a small, square door to find raised wooden boards covered with ferns for sleeping on, and a fire to keep them dry. He peered through an open-weave rush trellis window at the stout wooden palisade defences, and on the hills beyond noted neat rows of kumaras growing.

Roux and du Clesmeur described the chief's large greenstone tiki, or pendant, carved like the wooden house posts into a human face. They also admired the short clubs made of greenstone, and the chief's flute, trumpet and box to store ceremonial feathers.

At first, relations were friendly, but du Fresne unwisely put a high-ranking Maori in chains for stealing a musket. The Maoris saw this as slavery and planned revenge. When du Fresne and fifteen others went on a fishing trip, the Maoris drew their patu, killed and later ate them.

Roux now found himself in command, and swore vengeance. Gathering twenty-six men he marched on the Maori pa. The defenders threw water on the narrow path to make it slippery while their leaders climbed on to the fighting platform to hurl down spears. But the Frenchmen's well-aimed muskets killed the chiefs and routed the discouraged Maoris. A great many Maoris were killed but every Frenchman returned to his ship. The Frenchmen reported that the Maoris were savage cannibals; the Maoris thought the French were ill-mannered intruders.

Maori houses were rectangular, made of wood and thatch, and often had decorated lintels. Notice the small window and door in this drawing of a chief's house by Augustus Earle.

Whalers and missionaries

New Zealand is so large, and the number of Europeans living there was so small, that for the seventy years following Cook's first voyage, their influence varied very much from place to place. We should first consider why the early Europeans went to New Zealand, and then try to imagine what the Maoris might want from them.

The few ships coming to New Zealand in the early 1800s wanted to trade with the Maoris and to kill whales and seals. Whale oil, whalebone and seal skins fetched high prices in America and Britain, and the long journey was well worth while. Of course, whaling crews needed fresh food and water and so made a practice of calling at 'ports'. One of their favourites was Kororareka in the Bay of Islands where a Maori community provided pork and potatoes in exchange for muskets and iron. But the whaling crews, though they may have enjoyed their time ashore, did not settle permanently.

Samuel Marsden was an English missionary in Australia, where he was senior chaplain to the colony of New South Wales. In 1814 he arranged for a small group of twenty-one missionaries and their families to move permanently to the Bay of Islands in New Zealand. This was a bold venture, some would say foolhardy, for only six years before Maoris had killed everyone on board the visiting ship *Boyd* at Whangaroa. The reason for the settlement was to convert the Maoris to the Christian faith. The missionaries' early efforts were, however, unsuccessful. It was more than ten years before they converted even one Maori to Christianity.

The whalers and missionaries provided the Maoris with European goods, particularly muskets. A tribe whose warriors were armed with these awesome new weapons had a decided advantage over old rivals – at least until their rivals welcomed other European traders who could supply guns. Before guns were available casualties in Maori warfare were not heavy.

But with new weapons the number of deaths, and of slaves taken and eaten, greatly increased. Hilltop pa no longer gave the same protection and a severe defeat meant further revenge to restore a tribe's prestige. Nor was war the only cause of death. Living for so many centuries in such a remote country, Maoris had little resistance to European diseases. When they caught flu or measles they often died. Missionaries who came to save Maori souls instead gave them fatal diseases.

The miseries of warfare and disease, however, soon helped the missionaries to achieve their aims. Hongi, the leader of the Nga Puhi tribe, returned from his wars with many slaves, some of whom sought refuge with the missionaries. These slaves were prepared to listen to the new faith, and some became Christians. When they returned to their own people, they began to spread the new religion themselves. Sometimes missionaries were called upon to mediate between tribes at war. Because they were neutral their advice was often accepted and so both tribes could end a conflict without losing their prestige. Gradually, too, missionaries took over from the Maori priests the healing of the sick and wounded. Their skilled treatment won them much mana and respect.

It was not long before their success astonished even the most hopeful among the missionaries. The second baptism took place in 1828, but thereafter Christianity spread rapidly. Whether excited by the missionaries' religion or by the chance it offered of learning to read and write, even the chiefs were converted, and whole tribes followed suit. William Colenso, who had set up a small printing press, could hardly keep up with the Maoris' demand for bibles. Even remote tribes built chapels, bought bibles and begged for their own missionaries.

The missionaries next encouraged the Maoris to stop practising 'non-Christian' customs. Chiefs no longer married several wives, and wives were no longer expected to take their own lives when their chief died. Traditional singing and dancing as well as the art of wood carving began to die out because these arts were connected with the Maori religion. Many Maoris took European names when they were baptised Christians. By 1840, New Zealand was becoming peaceful and prosperous although there were still very few Europeans living there.

British settlers arrive

Occasional whaling and sealing boats and the missionaries changed much in Maori society, but did not lead to strife between Maori and Pakeha. But in 1837 a firm and much more dangerous step was taken. In distant England, Edward Wakefield formed the New Zealand Company, with plans to establish permanent settlements in New Plymouth, Wan-

ganui, Wellington and Nelson. These settlements would mirror English ways, with traders, artisans and farmers. However, all the areas proposed were occupied by powerful tribes, to whom English farming communities would be most unwelcome. Early in 1840, William Hobson arrived from New South Wales to be lieutenant-governor of the new British colony. His orders were to take over the colony in the name of the Crown, and to arrange a treaty with the Maori chiefs. A few weeks later, forty-five chiefs gathered at a great meeting and after much debate signed the Treaty of Waitangi. This treaty promised to protect the Maoris' rights to their land and other possessions, with the Crown alone having the right to buy Maori land. Maoris were given the same protection under the law as the British, provided they agreed that Queen

Maoris arriving for worship at the mission station at Whangaroa. A drawing made in 1846.

Victoria was their ruler. Te Kemara, a Ngati Kawa chief at the Waitangi debate, summed up the feelings of many other Maoris when he said: 'Government, go home and leave us to the Missionaries.'

Before 1840, New Zealand did not attract British colonists. It was distant, little known, and thought of as occupied by dangerous tribes. But after the Napoleonic Wars things changed and times became harder in Europe. There was poverty on the land and problems of crowding in the industrial towns. Soon a flood of settlers began to leave for New Zealand. Many were farmers, and they wanted land.

Now the Maori and European attitudes towards land were quite different, and neither fully appreciated the other's point of view. For the Maori, the tribal ownership of land is an ancestral right. It is a source of inspiration and pride, and can only be taken from him by force.

For the Pakehas, land can be parcelled up into lots, and sold to individuals. The new Pakeha farmers tried to win a livelihood by planting crops in every corner, and raising livestock. The more expensive the land, the more intensively it must be farmed. These farmers and land dealers bought land from the Maoris, often paying only a paltry sum. For their part the Maoris did not understand the full consequences of the trans-

action. When survey teams laid out pegs, and new settlers built houses and began ploughing, the Maoris took up arms.

Anglo-Maori wars

Fighting first came to Wairau in 1843, to the Bay of Islands, then spread to Taranaki, the Waikato, Wanganui and the Bay of Plenty. On their side, the British had the advantage of discipline, more resources and superior weapons. Occasionally, too, some Maoris would side with them against old tribal enemies. But the Maoris travelled light, knew the country, and adapted quickly to counter European tactics. While British commanders had their men transport huge siege guns to remote pa, the Maoris would strike fast, and disappear into the undergrowth. When the guns were finally in place, the defenders would slip away to another pa. In the picture above, you can see a typical engagement through the eyes of Sergeant Williams of the 68th regiment. A Maori pa lies in the middle distance, and in the foreground you can see a line of British troops with some Maori allies to the left. Some wounded soldiers lie down, and more are ascending to the hillock, limping along, or being carried. There is a small lake to the right, and fierce battle rages on the hillock above it.

The Omata Stockade, long deserted, lies beside the main road near New Plymouth. It once housed British troops. You can see them lined up in the picture below. Then, a horse-drawn cart and solitary horsemen used the road below the stockade.

This is what happened that day. The British colonel split his troops into two groups. One was to fire on the pa from the front and we see them doing that in the picture. They used naval rockets, but these were difficult to aim, and did little damage. The other group was ordered to seize the hillock and attack from the flank. Twice they were themselves assaulted by Maori war parties. On the first occasion the British drove the Maoris off with fixed bayonets. Sergeant Williams later drew the situation at three o'clock in the afternoon. A war party under chief Tupou has issued from the pa and is attacking a line of British troops. You can make them out, as they climb up from the pa to a long line of British soldiers. Each side then tried to drive the other into the lake, but the discipline of the British told, and the Maoris retreated to their pa.

In the wars which followed in Taranaki, the Waikato and the Bay of Plenty, each side struggled to win supremacy by developing new ways of fighting. In Taranaki, the Pakehas built stockades in the countryside as strong points in case of surprise attack. These pictures show the Omata Stockade as it was in 1860 and as it is today. The stockade was recently excavated by a team of archaeologists. They located the building foundations, musket balls, a button of the 57th regiment, and an ointment jar 'to cure ulcers, bad legs, sore breasts and sore heads, gout and rheumatism'. The jar came from the manufacturers at 224 The Strand, London.

During the wars, in 1858, several North Island tribes faced with a common enemy had come together and elected their own king. Not all tribes joined the king movement, but it strengthened resistance to the settlers and the army. Despite such desperate resistance, the British Army was too well equipped and well trained and defeated the Maoris. By 1865 only guerrilla groups in remote mountainous areas held out. In the rich farmland of the North Island, Maori resistance petered out and Pakeha farmers settled down to develop their newly won land.

8 Maoritanga

After the wars

The Maoris had gone to war with the Pakehas who had settled on their land. For centuries Maoris had fought each other over tribal ownership of land and now its loss to the Pakehas was deeply and sorely felt. Although they were united in their dislike of a common enemy, the tribes reacted differently to the new situation.

Maoris in the remoter country areas continued to farm but under Pakeha rule land was no longer held for the use of a whole tribe. Within a tribe's lands, individuals were allowed to own plots and even to sell them. So the land was broken up into small farms which could not be run efficiently. These relatively poor farmers lived in small whares, or houses, where conditions were hard and unhealthy. They still co-operated with each other at harvest, or mustering time. They spoke

Parihaka was a Maori settlement founded by the Taranaki leader Te Whiti. He shunned all contact with the Pakehas. This photograph, taken in November 1881, shows a meeting in progress at the right centre.

their own language and had little to do with Pakehas.

One such settlement was Parihaka in Taranaki. It was established on confiscated land soon after the wars by the leader Te Whiti. He and his followers cultivated the land round the village, and shunned contact with the Pakehas. He preached peace and goodwill, but when his followers plowed up pegs laid by a government survey team they were shown no mercy; the village was burned and Te Whiti arrested. In the Waikato area, support for the Maori king continued, and contact with the Pakehas was slight.

People in these country areas had little chance to influence the way the country was run. There were few schools and little was taught about the Maoris. The few Maori children who did go on to secondary school could only learn about the ways of the Pakehas who had recently defeated them and taken much of their land. They could not get the education they needed for well-paid and responsible jobs in Pakeha society and so they remained in their own isolated communities.

There were other Maoris, however, who took a different line: they preferred to co-operate with the government. In 1867, four Maori seats in parliament were established, and Maori men were given the vote. By 1883, all adult Maoris could vote; in Britain at this time, women were still not entitled to vote. In a society used to respecting men of learning and

above: *The end of the Anglo-Maori Wars were hard times for the rural Maoris. This village is Koroniti in Wanganui. Compare this photograph taken in the 1880s with the drawings on pages 31, 33 and 34.*

below: *Maori agriculture was often on a small scale. This harvesting scene was photographed in the 1890s in North Auckland. The sacks are full of kumaras.*

above: *Sir Apirana Ngata (1874–1950) stands at the centre of the picture as he opens the restoration of the Ngati Porou marae at Waiomatatini.*

right: *Sir Maui Pomare (1876–1930)*

far right: *Sir Peter Buck (1880–1951)*

mana, members of parliament, or Maoris who obtained Pakeha qualifications without losing their respect and concern for Maori welfare, achieved power and influence.

Sir Maui Pomare was one such leader. He was a qualified doctor, and worked hard to improve the health and welfare of the Maori people. Most rural whares had no water or sanitation. Child deaths and illness were much higher than among the mainly urban Pakehas. First as a health officer and then as the Minister of Health, Pomare saw that living standards were improved.

Sir Peter Buck trained as a doctor, and worked alongside Pomare in improving rural health care. But he was also a specialist in Maori culture and history, stressing, in his own words, that 'The importance of tribal loyalty, the marae (the meeting-house area) and the tangi (burial rite) are measures of our self respect.'

Another important leader was Sir Apirana Ngata who encouraged Maori farmers to join up their separate little small-holdings into bigger, single farms to make better use of the land. At the same time, he and his colleagues supported the building by tribal groups of their own marae as centres for their ceremonies.

Leaders like Pomare were also influential between the two World Wars in getting the Maori language and culture taught in schools alongside the usual Pakeha subjects. They encouraged opportunities for Maoris to go on to further students. Many Maoris fought in the Second World War where the Maori battalion was renowned for its courage. At the Battle of Alamein they performed a traditional haka, or war dance, before going into battle. As they had fought alongside Pakehas in war, so in peacetime they began to work alongside them in factories, teach and be taught by them in schools and universities, and sit with them in parliament.

The Maoris today

When the Pakehas took over Aotearoa, the Maoris' tribal leadership and customs did not entirely die out. The word that sums up the way the Maoris think of themselves, their tribes and their ancestors is Maoritanga. This is a difficult word to define but a good way to understand it is to take part in a hui, or Maori ceremony.

The hui will take place in the marae which is an open area of Maori land containing a meeting house for speech-making and sleeping, a cook house and a dining-hall. Hollows in the ground filled with charcoal and burned stones show where the hangi have been dug. All ceremonies, like funerals, weddings and 21st birthday celebrations, take place on marae.

Guests are welcomed on a Maori marae in the 1970s.

This time the occasion is a meeting between members of the Ngati Tehangi and a group of visitors who have come from all over New Zealand to discuss Maori attitudes towards archaeologists who wish to excavate old Maori living sites. The marae is about 6½ km (4 miles) from Tauranga, in the Bay of Plenty.

At eleven o'clock, the visitors line up, and walk into the open area in front of the meeting house. There is a gap of about 35 metres (115 feet) between them and their hosts. Both groups sit in lines on wooden benches facing each other.

After several minutes' silence, an elder stands and advances a few metres towards his guests. Quietly he welcomes the visitors in the Maori language. He refers to the ancestral spirits who are present, and, as his speech proceeds, his voice becomes louder, and his expressions are accompanied by hand gestures. Towards the end of his welcome, he breaks into a dignified dance, accompanied by the chanting of his fellow Maoris. As many of his guests do not speak Maori, he repeats some of his words in English for their benefit.

Then he resumes his seat and again there is silence. Now it is the guests' turn and one of their leaders stands to give thanks for the welcome. If the guest speaks even a few sentences in Maori, he immediately gains the respect of his hosts.

One by one, the Maori elders and principal guests respond to each others' speeches, but no one mentions the business at

This haka or war dance is part of a marae ceremony. The boy on the left is sticking his tongue out, just as the warriors did when Captain Cook arrived in 1769 (see the drawing on page 27)!

hand; that would be impolite, because the welcoming ceremony must take its course. After the last speech, the guests move in line to be personally welcomed by the Maoris. Some shake hands, but most adopt the Maori method of slowly rubbing noses.

The official opening ceremony is now complete and everyone proceeds to the dining-hall for lunch. There is plenty of food. Guests and hosts talk informally until the leaders move to the meeting house. When everyone is assembled in front, the speakers begin to discuss the business. The visitors explain why they wish to excavate old sites: how it is possible to learn about the way of life of the ancestors in Aotearoa, and how they can increase understanding of their great achievements. Then the Maori elders talk about the tapu, or sacredness, which surrounds their ancient sites. The hui lasts two days. Food is cooked on electric stoves in the cookhouse and for the ceremonial farewell meal, in a hangi. A Pakeha

meeting would involve a chairman, a formal agenda, and would only last a few hours. But here farewells, too, are accompanied by further speeches from the hosts, and responses from the senior guests.

Most Maoris deeply value the importance of their tribal heritage and their association with sacred places. Where a Pakeha will see a beach, a headland and ridgetops, the Maoris will see a headland with an ancestral pa, a ridgetop with a burial ground and a beach where his tribe's founding canoe landed. Maoritanga has survived the coming of the Europeans and two centuries of living with the Pakeha. It continues as a distinctive but essential part of New Zealand culture.

Glossary of Maori Words

Aotearoa—the Maori name for the country now known as New Zealand

haka—a war dance

hangi—a pit lined with hot stones in which food was cooked; an earth oven

hapu—a segment of a large tribe, related by blood or by marriage

hinau—a tree whose berries, bark, and gum were used to make dyes and pigments

hui—a Maori ceremony

kakawai—a fish found in the coastal waters of Aotearoa

karaka—a tree whose berries and kernels were eaten by the Maori

kumaras—sweet potatoes

mana—prestige or moral authority. A person possessing high mana was treated with awe and respect.

Maoritanga—the Maoris' feeling about their heritage and culture

marae—an open area in a Maori settlement used for meetings and ceremonies

mere—a type of stabbing club

moa—a large flightless bird, now extinct

muru—a system of punishment used against Maoris who broke tribal rules

nikau—a kind of palm tree

pa—a fortified village

Pakehas—the Maori word for strangers or foreigners

pipi—a kind of shellfish

puke—a small mound of earth used to protect growing kumaras

tangi—a burial rite

tapu—something sacred or dangerous; also the prohibition against going to a tapu place or interfering with a person who is tapu. The English word *taboo* comes from the Maori *tapu*.

Tainui—one of the canoes in which, according to legend, the Maoris first reached Aotearoa

Te Arawa—another of the legendary canoes of the Maori past

tiki—an image of a supernatural being, often worn as a pendant

tohunga ahurewa—priests responsible for memorizing sacred chants that recorded Maori history and religious beliefs

totara—a large tree used to make canoe hulls

utu—revenge taken against someone who insulted an individual or a tribe

whares—houses

Archaeologists often find earth ovens, or hangi, like this one. You can see the hollow of the pit cut into the sand.

Index

Acknowledgments

Illustrations in this book are reproduced by kind permission of the following:
p 5 Mitchell Library, Sydney; pp 7, 29, 30, 44, 45 (below) Alexander Turnbull Library, Wellington; pp 8, 43 N. Prickett, Anthropology Department, University of Auckland; p 10 Department of Lands and Survey, New Zealand; pp 12 (right), 19, 24 (top centre) B. F. Leach; pp 13 (left), 14, 24 (top right), 32, 39 (top, centre) Otago Museum; p 13 (right) E. F. E. Higham; p 18 Whites Aviation Auckland; pp 24 (top left), 25, 26 C. F. W. Higham; pp 24 (below left), 47, 48 Dr Ann Salmond; pp 27, 28 reproduced by permission of the British Library Board; pp 31, 33, 34 (below), 39 (below) Rex Nan Kivell Collection, National Library of Australia; p 36 Faculty of Archaeology and Anthropology, Cambridge; p 41 The Methodist Church Overseas Division; pp 42, 45 (top), 46 (centre, right) Hocken Library Dunedin; p 46 (left) Gisborne Museum and Arts Centre

Reconstruction drawings by Murray Webb
Maps and diagrams by Reg Piggott, Richard Newall, Martin Fisher

front and back cover: *From 'New Zealanders Illustrated' by G. F. Angas, published in 1847; see page 35 for the frontispiece. The front cover shows the house of Hiwikau, and the back cover Te Ngaporutu with his wife.*

The Cambridge History Library

The Cambridge Introduction to History
Written by Trevor Cairns

PEOPLE BECOME CIVILIZED

THE ROMANS AND THEIR EMPIRE

BARBARIANS, CHRISTIANS, AND MUSLIMS

THE MIDDLE AGES

EUROPE AROUND THE WORLD

EUROPE AND THE WORLD

THE BIRTH OF MODERN EUROPE

THE OLD REGIME AND THE REVOLUTION

POWER FOR THE PEOPLE

The Cambridge Topic Books
General Editor Trevor Cairns

THE AMERICAN WAR OF INDEPENDENCE

BENIN: AN AFRICAN KINGDOM AND CULTURE

THE BUDDHA

BUILDING THE MEDIEVAL CATHEDRALS

CHINA AND MAO ZEDONG

CHRISTOPHER WREN
AND ST. PAUL'S CATHEDRAL

THE EARLIEST FARMERS AND THE FIRST CITIES

EARLY CHINA AND THE WALL

THE FIRST SHIPS AROUND THE WORLD

GANDHI AND THE STRUGGLE
FOR INDIA'S INDEPENDENCE

HERNAN CORTES: CONQUISTADOR IN MEXICO

HITLER AND THE GERMANS

THE INDUSTRIAL REVOLUTION BEGINS

LIFE IN A FIFTEENTH-CENTURY MONASTERY

LIFE IN A MEDIEVAL VILLAGE

LIFE IN THE IRON AGE

LIFE IN THE OLD STONE AGE

THE MAORIS

MARTIN LUTHER

MEIJI JAPAN

THE MURDER OF ARCHBISHOP THOMAS

MUSLIM SPAIN

THE NAVY THAT BEAT NAPOLEON

THE PARTHENON

POMPEII

THE PYRAMIDS

THE ROMAN ARMY

THE ROMAN ENGINEERS

ST. PATRICK AND IRISH CHRISTIANITY

THE VIKING SHIPS

The Cambridge History Library will be expanded in the future to include additional volumes. Lerner Publications Company is pleased to participate in making this excellent series of books available to a wide audience of readers.

Lerner Publications Company
241 First Avenue North, Minneapolis, Minnesota 55401